The Magdalena Prayer Book

DEVOTIONS FOR

Habitual Perfect Contrition

AND

Spiritual Communion

Presented by Gaudent Angeli

SOPHIA INSTITUTE PRESS
Manchester, New Hampshire

Cover by Gaudent Angeli and Steven Nelson

Cover image: *Christ's Appearance to Mary Magdalene after the Resurrection*, painting (1585) by Alexander Andreyevich Ivanov

Sophia Institute Press
Box 5284, Manchester, NH 03108
1-800-888-9344
www.SophiaInstitute.com

Sophia Institute Press is a registered trademark of Sophia Institute.

paperback ISBN: 979-8-88911-196-2
ebook ISBN: 979-8-88911-197-9

Library of Congress Control Number: TO COME

First printing

In Rememberance

Of those good men and women who established the One True Faith, and thereby the Mercy of God, in the new world. May they rest in peace. Amen.

Dedicated To

The renewal of Catholic faith & culture in Los Angeles, California, the Americas, and the world.

Contents

The Magdalena Prayer Book

Introduction

"And he that sat on the throne, said: Behold, I make all things new. And he said to me: Write, for these words are most faithful and true."

Christ in Glory to His Beloved Apostle,
Apocalypse 21:5

In this handbook, you are invited to deepen and develop the habit of perfect contrition for past and present sins through prayer, and unite spiritually to the Most Holy Eucharist as often as possible throughout the day.

The title for *The Magdalena Prayer Book* comes from the Queen of Penitents herself: St. Mary Magdalene[1]. During her earthly life, this woman perfectly illustrated the path of true and perfect contrition, and has been the model soul for those in mortal sin who thirst for forgiveness.

This book serves to stand in the breach, so to speak, and provide devotions that might supplement the life of the repentant sinner if he finds himself in the unfortunate state of mortal sin, while the opportunity for Confession is in short supply.

All theology presented herein is based on the timeless instruction of the Council of Trent and the Roman Catechism (i.e., The Catechism of the Council of Trent).

All scripture references are from the Douay-Rheims 1899 American Edition. All errors are human, all Glory is the Lord's.

Holy Mary, Queen of Angels,
Mother of Mercy, pray for us!

St. Vibiana, Virgin and Martyr,
Patroness of Los Angeles, pray for us!

Deo Optimo Maximo,
Gaudent Angeli Team

WRITTEN ON THE FEAST OF THE MARTYR,
POPE ST. SIXTUS II
AUGUST 7TH, A.D. 2020

---

1. Gaudent Angeli subscribes to the magisterial teaching of Pope St. Gregory the Great and the perennial liturgical prayers of the Catholic Church (*Lex Orandi Lex Credendi*), that the woman who annointed Christ twice before his death, who was the sister of Ss. Martha and Lazarus of Bethany, and to whom our Lord appeared when he rose again, is the same woman: St. Mary Magdalene. For further reading, see *St. Mary Magdalene* by Fr. Sean Davidson.

A Short Treatise on Perfect Contrition & Spiritual Communion

According to the Council of Trent

What is Contrition?

"The penitent, through perfect contrition, accompanied by the desire of confession, has already obtained remission of his sins from God."

Roman Catechism,
Part 2, Section 4, Penance

The idea of contrition is very unique to the Roman Catholic Tradition. The word itself literally means "the breaking of an object into small parts by means of a stone or some harder substance; and here it is used metaphorically, to signify that our hearts, hardened by pride, are beaten and broken by penance." (*Ibid., The First Part of Penance*) It follows then that contrition has to do with the heart, and the heart's relation to sin and conversion to God.

The Catechism of the Council of Trent thoroughly and timelessly defines contrition as "a sorrow and detestation for sin committed, with a purpose of sinning no more.... If joined with a confidence in the mercy of God and an earnest desire of performing whatever is necessary to the proper reception of the Sacrament, it thus prepares us for the remission of sin." (*Ibid., The First Part of Penance*)

Perfect contrition is, as the name implies, the perfect movement of contrition in the soul. This is only possible with God's help, and has the ability to pardon our sins even before we go to Confession. Although Sacramental Confession is to be encouraged and sought as our ordinary means of forgiveness, in times when the sacraments are scarce, we must pray frequently to obtain perfect contrition.

It is when we have sorrow and detestation for sin committed, "because thou art all good and deserving of all my love," as the Act of Contrition says, that contrition is mobilized to perfection. This is distinct from imperfect contrition, which Trent describes as "attrition, since it commonly arises either from the consideration of the heinousness of sin or from the fear of hell and of punishment." (*Council of Trent, Section 14, Ch 4, Contrition*)

How to Evoke Contrition

"Contrition is evoked by examination, recollection, and hatred of sins."

Council of Trent,
Section 14, Penance Canon 5

Though God's help is necessary to move our hearts to perfect contrition, we can do our part to prepare to receive His grace and mercy by a thorough self-examination. Trent admonished clergy to remind the lay faithful,

> frequently to examine their consciences, in order to ascertain if they have been faithful in the observance of those things which God and His Church require. Should anyone be conscious of sin, he should immediately accuse himself, humbly solicit pardon from God, and implore time to confess and satisfy for his sins. Above all, let him supplicate the aid of divine grace, in order that he may not relapse into those sins which he now penitently deplores. (*Ibid.*)

Without examining ourselves often, we cannot know ourselves, and we cannot truly encounter our sins and see them as God wants us to see them. For some, the periodic or frequent examination of conscience might invoke fear and trepidation. Facing our faults can be daunting. But we must remember: God wants to save us.

Trent softens the blow, and further elaborates on the real possibility of attaining perfect contrition:

> for since God is most desirous of our salvation, He will not delay to pardon us. With a father's fondness, He embraces the sinner the moment he enters into himself, turns to the Lord and, having detested all his sins, resolves that later on, as far as he is able, he will call them singly to mind and confess them. The Almighty Himself, by the mouth of His Prophet, commands us to hope, when He says: The wickedness of the wicked shall not hurt him, in what day soever he shall turn from his wickedness. (*Roman Catechism, Part 2, Section 4, The First Part of Penance*)

The following is a detailed anatomy of the conditions required for perfect contrition and spiritual communion.

Anatomy of Perfect Contrition & Spiritual Communion

According to the Council of Trent

I. Love of God
II. Hatred of Sin and Necessity of Sorrow
III. Intention to Confess and Satisfy
IV. The Will to Amend
V. Confidence in Divine Mercy
VI. Spiritual Communion

I. Love of God

"God is to be loved above all things, and whatever separates us from God is therefore to be hated above all things. It is also worthy of note that to charity and contrition the language of Scripture assigns the same extent. Of charity it is said: Thou shalt love the Lord thy God with thy whole heart. Of contrition the Lord says through the Prophet: Be converted with your whole heart."

Roman Catechism
Part 2, Section 4, The First Part of Penance

"That God is to be loved above all things, so that we should be prepared to sacrifice our lives rather than offend Him, these words of the Lord clearly declare: He that loveth father or mother more than me, is not worthy of me; He that will save his life shall lose it."

Ibid.

II. Hatred of Sin and Necessity of Sorrow

"Intense hatred and a lively detestation of past transgressions."

Ibid.

"The sorrow with which we are overwhelmed by the forfeiture of the grace of God and of our own innocence."

Ibid.

"...must exclude all apathy and indifference."

Ibid.

"If our sorrow and detestation extend only to some sins, our repentance is not salutary, but feigned and false."

Ibid.

III. Intention to Confess and Satisfy

"Our contrition must be accompanied with a desire of confessing and satisfying [doing penance] for our sins."

Ibid.

IV. The Will to Amend

WILLINGNESS TO DO PENANCE

"Be converted and do penance for all your iniquities, and iniquity shall not be your ruin. Cast away from you

all your transgressions, by which you have transgressed, and make yourselves a new heart and a new spirit."

Ezekiel 18:30-31

THE DECISION TO SIN NO MORE

"Then Jesus lifting up himself, said to her: Woman, where are they that accused thee? Hath no man condemned thee? Who said: No man, Lord. And Jesus said: Neither will I condemn thee. Go, and now sin no more. Again therefore, Jesus spoke to them, saying: I am the light of the world: he that followeth me, walketh not in darkness, but shall have the light of life."

John 8:10-12

IF NECESSARY, RESTITUTION

"If, therefore, by force or fraud, the penitent has taken anything from his neighbour, he is bound to restitution. Likewise if, by word or deed, he has injured his neighbour's honour or reputation, he is under an obligation of repairing the injury by procuring him some advantage or rendering him some service. Well known to all is the maxim of St. Augustine: The sin is not forgiven unless what has been taken away is restored."

Roman Catechism
Part 2, Section 4, The First Part of Penance

IF NECESSARY, FORGIVENESS OF INJURIES

"Again, not less necessary for contrition than the other chief conditions is a care that it be accompanied by entire forgiveness of the injuries which we may have received from others. This our Lord and Saviour admonishes when He declares: If you will forgive men their offences, your heavenly Father will forgive you also your offences, but if you will not forgive men, neither will your Father forgive you your offences."

Ibid.

V. Confidence in Divine Mercy

"But lest the faithful, terrified by the grievousness of their sins, despair of being able to obtain pardon, the pastor ought to encourage them to hope by the following considerations.... Christ the Lord has given power to the Church to remit sins. Furthermore...our Lord has taught how great is the goodness and bounty of God towards mankind; for if God were not ready and prepared to pardon penitents their sins, never would He have prescribed this formula of prayer: Forgive us our trespasses. Wherefore we ought to be firmly convinced, that since He commands us in this petition to implore His paternal mercy, He will not fail to bestow it on us.

For this petition assuredly implies that God is so disposed towards us, as willingly to pardon those who are truly penitent."

Roman Catechism
Our Father, Chapter 4, Section 5

VI. Spiritual Communion

"As to the use of this holy sacrament, our Fathers have rightly and wisely distinguished three ways of receiving it. They have taught that some receive it sacramentally only, as sinners; others spiritually only, namely, those who in desiring the heavenly bread set before them, are by a lively 'faith which worketh by charity' made sensible of its fruit and usefulness; while the third class receives it both sacramentally and spiritually, and these are they who so prove and prepare themselves beforehand that they approach this divine table clothed with the wedding garment."

Council of Trent
Session 13, Section 8, Use Of

Spiritual Communion is the reception of the Eucharist in spirit only. Also called the "communion of desire," this form of reception is made possible by prayer, and is encouraged by the Church to be frequented often, in hopes of receiving the grace and benefits of the Blessed Sacrament while being deprived of the sacramental species themselves (the consecrated bread and wine).

It is worth noting that receiving the Eucharist requires us to be properly disposed. Most importantly, it requires the State of Grace. Or, as Trent applies above to Sacramental Communion: "prove and prepare.... beforehand that they approach this divine table clothed with the wedding garment." To a degree, this is true for Spiritual Communion also.

As Trent declares, those who receive it spiritually only, "are by a lively 'faith which worketh by charity' made sensible of its fruit and usefulness." Since charity requires sanctifying grace, the fruits of Spiritual Communion will not be imparted to the communicant if they are without grace to make the communion happen.

Still, since our reception is spiritual only, and since "the Spirit breatheth where he will" (John 3:8), the spiritual communicant who finds himself in mortal sin, but having contrition, may make spiritual communions and not commit sin/sacrilige, hoping for the requisite graces to come from our benevolent God, and thereby dispose him to receive our Lord in a spiritual manner.

In my affliction I called upon the Lord, and I cried to my God. And he heard my voice from his holy temple and my cry before him came into his ears.

He sent from on high, and took me and received me out of many waters.

And he brought me forth into a large place; he saved me, because he was well pleased with me.

PSALM 17:7,17,20

Devotions

I. Love of God

"God is to be loved above all things, and whatever separates us from God is therefore to be hated above all things."

Roman Catechism

The *Memorare*

Remember, O most gracious Virgin Mary, that never was it known that anyone who fled to thy protection, implored thy help, or sought thy intercession was left unaided. Inspired with this confidence, I fly to thee, O Virgin of virgins, my Mother; to thee do I come; before thee I stand, sinful and sorrowful. O Mother of the Word Incarnate, despise not my petitions, but in thy mercy hear and answer me. Amen.

Memoráre, o piísima Virgo María, non esse audítum a saéculo, quémquam ad tua curréntem præsídia, tua implorántem auxília, tua peténtem suffrágia, esse derelíctum. Ego, tali animátus confidéntia ad te, Virgo Vírginum Mater, curro, ad te vénio; coram te gémens peccátor assísto. Noli, Mater Verbi, verba mea despícere, sed audi propítia et exáudi. Amen.

Prayer Before a Crucifix

Look down upon me, good and gentle Jesus, while before Thy face I humbly kneel; and with burning soul, I pray and beseech Thee to fix deep in my heart lively sentiments of faith, hope, and charity; true contrition for my sins; and a firm purpose of amendment.

While I contemplate, with great love and tender pity, Thy five most precious wounds, pondering over them within me and calling to mind the words which David, Thy prophet, said of Thee, my Jesus: "They have pierced My hands and My feet, they have numbered all My bones." Amen.

Psalm 50

Miserere
The Fourth Penitential Psalm

Have mercy on me, O God,
according to thy great mercy.
And according to the multitude of thy tender
mercies, blot out my iniquity.

Wash me yet more from my iniquity,
and cleanse me from my sin.

For I know my iniquity,
and my sin is always before me.

To thee only have I sinned,
and have done evil before thee:
that thou mayst be justified in thy words,
and mayst overcome when thou art judged.

For behold I was conceived in iniquities;
and in sins did my mother conceive me.

For behold thou hast loved truth:
the uncertain and hidden things
of thy wisdom thou hast made
manifest to me.

Thou shalt sprinkle me with hyssop,
and I shall be cleansed:
thou shalt wash me,
and I shall be made
whiter than snow.

To my hearing thou shalt give
joy and gladness: and the bones
that have been humbled
shall rejoice.

Turn away thy face from my sins,
and blot out all my iniquities.

Create a clean heart in me, O God:
and renew a right spirit within my bowels.

Cast me not away from thy face;
and take not thy holy spirit from me.

Restore unto me the joy of thy salvation,
and strengthen me with a perfect spirit.

Collect for the Feast of St. Peter in Chains

O God, You freed the blessed apostle Peter from his chains and sent him forth unharmed. Free us from the bonds of our sins and in Your mercy shield us from all harm. Through Christ our Lord. Amen.

Act of Love

O my God, I love Thee with my whole heart and soul, and above all things, because Thou art infinitely good and perfect and most worthy of all my love; and, for Thy sake, I love my neighbour as myself. Mercifully grant, O my God, that having loved Thee on earth, I may love and enjoy Thee forever in Heaven. Amen.

Act of Contrition

O my God, I am heartily sorry for having offended Thee, and I detest all my sins, because I dread the loss of Heaven, and the pains of Hell;

But most of all because they offend Thee, my God, Who art all good and deserving of all my love.

I firmly resolve, with the help of Thy grace,

To confess my sins, to do penance, and to amend my life.

Amen.

VI. Hatred of Sin

"It must exclude all apathy and indifference."

Roman Catechism

The Prayer of Manasseh

O Lord Almighty, God of our fathers Abraham, Isaac, and Jacob, and of all their righteous seed;

O Lord Thou who hast made heaven and earth with all their adornments;

Thou who hast marked the sea with Thy word of command, Thou who hast confined the deep and marked it with Thy terrible and glorious name; at Whom all things quake and tremble before the face of Thy power, for unbearable is the majesty of Thy glory and overwhelming is the threat of Thy wrath upon sinners;

Yet truly immeasurable and unsearchable is the promise of Thy mercy, for Thou art the Lord, the Most High over all the earth, compassionate, long-suffering, full of mercy, and lamenting over the evils of men.

But Thou, O Lord, according to Thy goodness, hast promised repentance and forgiveness for those who have sinned against Thee; and in the multitude of Thy mercies Thou hast appointed repentance for salvation of sinners.

Therefore, Thou, O Lord, God of the just, hast not appointed repentance for Abraham, Isaac, and Jacob, who did not sin against Thee, but Thou hast appointed penance for me on account of my sins.

For my sins number more than the grains of sand in the sea, my sins I have multiplied, O Lord, my sins I have multiplied! I am not worthy to gaze upon and behold heaven above because of the multitude of my sins.

I am bowed down by many fetters of iron, so that I cannot lift my head nor can I breathe, for I have provoked Thy wrath and done evil in Thy sight, setting up abominations and multiplying my offenses.

And now I bend my knee and humble my heart, beseeching Thy goodness, O Lord.

I have sinned, O Lord, I have sinned, and I acknowledge my transgressions.

For this reason I beg to ask Thee,

O Lord, forgive me, forgive me! Do not destroy me with my transgressions nor be angry forever with me nor condemn me to the depths of the inferno.

For I say Thou art, O God, the God of the repentant, and in me Thou wilt show Thy great goodness! For, unworthy as I am, Thou wilt save me according to Thy great mercy, and I will praise Thee always for all of the days of my life. For all the host of the heavens praise Thee and to Thee be glory forever. Amen.

(Appendixed prayer of the Latin Vulgate, attributed to King Manasseh in 2 Chr 33:13)

Examination of Conscience

1. I am the Lord thy God, who brought thee out of the land of Egypt, out of the house of bondage. Thou shalt not have strange gods before me. Thou shalt not make to thyself a graven thing, nor the likeness of any thing that is in heaven above, or in the earth beneath, nor of those things that are in the waters under the earth. Thou shalt not adore them, nor serve them.

(Have I doubted in matters of faith, murmured against God, committed acts of superstition, encouraged heresy? Have I received Holy Communion in a state of mortal sin?)

2. Thou shalt not take the name of the Lord thy God in vain.

(Have I represented the faith falsely or for vain reasons, used the name of God or the Saints as swear words, not made reparation for those that do?)

3. Remember thou keep holy the Sabbath day.

(Have I assisted at Mass per the Sunday obligation? Neglected to sanctify the day if I could not attend Mass?

Performed or requested unnecessary servile work or commerce?)

4. Honor thy father and thy mother.

(Have I shown due honor, love, gratitude, and obedience to my parents and or superiors? Failed to practice patriotic duties when required of me? Spoke ill of, or exposed the faults of, pastors or the Pope? Neglected devotion to the Blessed Virgin Mary?)

5. Thou shalt not kill.

(Have I unjustly killed another human being? Wished he/she were dead or harbored resentment and anger toward him/her in my heart? Have I taken care of my body and not overindulged its desire for pleasure? Have I driven intoxicated or in a way that I put someone's life in danger, including my own?)

6 & 9. Thou shalt not commit adultery. Thou shalt not covet thy neighbor's wife.

(Have I entertained thoughts, glances, or actions that do not protect my purity or the purity of others? Masturbated? Have I been guilty of using pornographic or immodest imagery and videos? If married, have I refused a reasonable request to fulfill the marital debt? Have I used artificial contraception or engaged in abortion?)

7 & 10. Thou shalt not steal. Thou shalt not covet thy neighbor's goods.

(Have I stolen or retained ill-gotten goods? Damaged or wasted the property of others? Accepted bribes? Neglected to make restitution, or to help the poor? Have I desired the goods of someone else?)

8. Thou shalt not bear false witness against thy neighbor.

(Have I spread unkind remarks others make to me? Do I discuss the faults of my parents, wife, husband, or children with others who have no business knowing anything about them? Have I lied or withheld the truth?)

Psalm 6

Domine, ne in furore I
The First Penitential Psalm

O Lord, rebuke me not in thy indignation, nor chastise me in thy wrath.

Have mercy on me, O Lord, for I am weak: heal me, O Lord, for my bones are troubled.

And my soul is troubled exceedingly: but thou, O Lord, how long?

Turn to me, O Lord, and deliver my soul: O save me for thy mercy's sake.

For there is no one in death, that is mindful of thee: and who shall confess to thee in hell?

I have laboured in my groanings, every night I will wash my bed: I will water my couch with my tears.

My eye is troubled through indignation: I have grown old amongst all my enemies.

Depart from me, all ye workers of iniquity: for the Lord hath heard the voice of my weeping.

The Lord hath heard my supplication: the Lord hath received my prayer.

Let all my enemies be ashamed, and be very much troubled: let them be turned back, and be ashamed very speedily.

Gradual for the Feast of the Beheading of St. John the Baptist

The just man shall flourish like the palm tree, like a cedar of Lebanon shall he grow in the house of the Lord.

To proclaim Your kindness at dawn and Your faithfulness thoughout the night. Alleluia, alleluia.

The just shall blossom like the lily; and flourish forever before the Lord. Alleluia.

Psalm 37

Domine, ne in furore II
The Third Penitential Psalm

Rebuke me not, O Lord, in thy indignation;
nor chastise me in thy wrath.

For thy arrows are fastened in me:
and thy hand hath been strong upon me.

There is no health in my flesh, because of thy
wrath: there is no peace for my bones, because
of my sins.

For my iniquities are gone over my head:
and as a heavy burden are become heavy upon me.

My sores are putrified and corrupted,
because of my foolishness.

I am become miserable, and am bowed down even
to the end: I walked sorrowful all the day long.

For my loins are filled with illusions;
and there is no health in my flesh.

I am afflicted and humbled exceedingly:
I roared with the groaning of my heart.

Lord, all my desire is before thee,
and my groaning is not hidden from thee.

My heart is troubled, my strength hath left me,
and the light of my eyes itself is not with me.

My friends and my neighbours have drawn near, and stood against me. And they that were near me stood afar off:

And they that sought my soul used violence. And they that sought evils to me spoke vain things, and studied deceits all the day long.

But I, as a deaf man, heard not:
and as a dumb man not opening his mouth.

And I became as a man that heareth not:
and that hath no reproofs in his mouth.

For in thee, O Lord, have I hoped:
thou wilt hear me, O Lord my God.

For I said: Lest at any time my enemies rejoice over me: and whilst my feet are moved, they speak great things against me.

For I am ready for scourges:
and my sorrow is continually before me.

For I will declare my iniquity:
and I will think for my sin.

But my enemies live, and are stronger that I:
and they hate me wrongfully are multiplied.

They that render evil for good, have detracted me,
because I followed goodness.

Forsake me not, O Lord my God:
do not thou depart from me.

Attend unto my help, O Lord,
the God of my salvation.

Act of Contrition

O my God, I am heartily sorry for having offended Thee, and I detest all my sins, because I dread the loss of Heaven, and the pains of Hell;

But most of all because they offend Thee, my God, Who art all good and deserving of all my love.

I firmly resolve, with the help of Thy grace,

To confess my sins, to do penance, and to amend my life.

Amen.

III. Intention to Confess and Satisfy

"Our contrition must be accompanied with a desire of confessing and satisfying [doing penance] for our sins."
Roman Catechism

Psalm 31

Beati quorum.
The Second Penitential Psalm

Blessed are they whose iniquities are forgiven,
and whose sins are covered.

Blessed is the man to whom the Lord hath not
inputed sin, and in whose spirit there is no guile.

Because I was silent my bones grew old;
whilst I cried out all the day long.

For day and night thy hand was heavy upon me:
I am turned in my anguish, whilst the thorn is
fastened.

I have acknowledged my sin to thee, and my
injustice I have not concealed. I said I will confess
against myself my injustice to the Lord: and thou
hast forgiven the wickedness of my sin.

For this shall every one that is holy pray to thee
in a seasonable time.

And yet in a flood of many waters,
they shall not come nigh unto him.

Thou art my refuge from the trouble which hath encompassed me: my joy, deliver me from them that surround me.

I will give thee understanding, and I will instruct thee in this way, in which thou shalt go:
I will fix my eyes upon thee.

Do not become like the horse and the mule, who have no understanding. With bit and bridle bind fast their jaws, who come not near unto thee.

Many are the scourges of the sinner, but mercy shall encompass him that hopeth in the Lord.
Be glad in the Lord, and rejoice, ye just, and glory, all ye right of heart.

Eastern Christian Hymn to Saint David, Prophet and King of Israel

When Nathan the prophet denounced David for his sin, he declared unto him the sentence of the Lord, saying: "I will raise up evil against thee out of thine own house, and the sword shall never depart from thee." And the words of the Lord were fulfilled in David's sons, Absalom and Amnon; for the one slew the other, and fled, and rose up against his father, to usurp his throne; and David in sadness was compelled to abandon Jerusalem his city. Yet was his trust in the Lord his God, and he did not cease to chant continually:

Alleluia!

David departed from Jerusalem, and Absalom, his son, entered the city and the king's palace, and set himself up to rule in his stead; and he dishonored his father's house. And this unworthy son dared also to assemble a mighty army to pursue his father, and there was a great battle, and Joab the general slew the hapless rebel; but David, when he heard this, covered his face, and wept bitterly, saying: "O Absalom, my son, my son Absalom! Would God I had died for thee, O Absalom, my son, my son!"

Wherefore, marvelling at thy paternal love, we cry to thee: Rejoice, for thou didst acknowledge the evil which thou hadst done before God;

Rejoice, for He restored unto thee the joy of His salvation! Rejoice, for with His governing Spirit did He establish thee;

Rejoice, for thou didst teach transgressors the ways of the Lord! Rejoice, for through thy zeal did the ungodly turn back unto Him;

Rejoice, for the Most High delivered thee from thy blood-guiltiness! Rejoice, for thy tongue rejoiceth in His righteousness;

Rejoice, for He opened thy lips, and thy mouth declared His praise! Rejoice, for thy broken spirit was a sacrifice unto God;

Rejoice, for thy contrite and humbled heart did He not despise! Rejoice, for in His good pleasure the Lord did good unto Sion;

Rejoice, for He was pleased with thy sacrifice of righteousness, with thine oblation and whole-burnt offerings!

Rejoice, O holy king and prophet David, thou ancestor of God and singer of His praises!

Psalm 101

Domine, exaudi
The Fifth Penitential Psalm

Hear, O Lord, my prayer:
and let my cry come to thee.

Turn not away thy face from me:
in the day when I am in trouble,
incline thy ear to me.

In what day soever I shall call upon thee,
hear me speedily.

For my days are vanished like smoke, and my bones are grown dry like fuel for the fire.

I am smitten as grass, and my heart is withered:
because I forgot to eat my bread.

Through the voice of my groaning,
my bone hath cleaved to my flesh.

I am become like to a pelican of the wilderness:
I am like a night raven in the house.

I have watched, and am become as a sparrow all
alone on the housetop.

All the day long my enemies reproached me:
and they that praised me did swear against me.

For I did eat ashes like bread,
and mingled my drink with weeping.

Because of thy anger and indignation:
for having lifted me up thou hast thrown me down.

My days have declined like a shadow,
and I am withered like grass.

But thou, O Lord, endurest for ever:
and thy memorial to all generations.

Thou shalt arise and have mercy on Sion: for it is
time to have mercy on it, for the time is come.

For the stones thereof have pleased thy servants:
and they shall have pity on the earth thereof.

All the Gentiles shall fear thy name, O Lord,
and all the kings of the earth thy glory.

For the Lord hath built up Sion:
and he shall be seen in his glory.

He hath had regard to the prayer of the humble: and he hath not despised their petition.

Let these things be written unto another generation: and the people that shall be created shall praise the Lord:

Because he hath looked forth from his high sanctuary: from heaven the Lord hath looked upon the earth.

That he might hear the groans of them that are in fetters: that he might release the children of the slain.

That they may declare the name of the Lord in Sion: and his praise in Jerusalem.

When the people assemble together, and kings, to serve the Lord.

He answered him in the way of his strength: Declare unto me the fewness of my days.

Call me not away in the midst of my days: thy years are unto generation and generation.

In the beginning, O Lord, thou foundedst the earth: and the heavens are the works of thy hands.

They shall perish but thou remainest: and all of
them shall grow old like a garment:

And as a vesture thou shalt change them,
and they shall be changed.

But thou art always the selfsame,
and thy years shall not fail.

The children of thy servants shall continue
and their seed shall be directed for ever.

Collect from the Feast of St. Mary Magdalene

May the prayers of blessed Mary Magdalene help us, O Lord, Who were moved by her prayers and brought back alive from the grave her brother Lazarus, dead for four days. Through Christ our Lord.

Lesson

CANTICLES 3:2-5, 8:6-7

I will rise and go about the city; in the streets and crossings I will seek Him Whom my heart loves. I sought Him but I did not find Him.

The watchmen came upon me as they made their rounds of the city: Have you seen Him Whom my heart loves? I had hardly left them when I found Him Whom my heart loves.

I took hold of Him and would not let Him go till I should bring Him to the home of my mother, to the room of my parent, I adjure you, daughters of

Jerusalem, by the gazelles and hinds of the field, do not arouse, do not stir up love before its own time.

Set me as a seal on Your heart, as a seal on Your arm; for stern as death is love, relentless as the nether world is devotion; its flames are a blazing fire.

Deep waters cannot quench love, nor floods sweep it away. Were one to offer all he owns to purchase love, he would despise it as nothing.

Act of Contrition

O my God, I am heartily sorry for having offended Thee, and I detest all my sins, because I dread the loss of Heaven, and the pains of Hell;

But most of all because they offend Thee, my God, Who art all good and deserving of all my love.

I firmly resolve, with the help of Thy grace,

To confess my sins, to do penance, and to amend my life.

Amen.

IV. The Will to Amend

"Be converted and do penance for all your iniquities, and iniquity shall not be your ruin."

The Holy Prophet Ezekiel

Litany of Penance

ST. JOHN HENRY NEWMAN

V. Lord, have mercy on us.

R. Christ, have mercy on us.

V. Lord, have mercy on us.

V. Christ, hear us.

R. Christ, graciously hear us.

God the Father of Heaven,
have mercy on us.

God the Son, Redeemer of the world,
have mercy on us.

God the Holy Ghost, have mercy on us.

Holy Trinity, one God, have mercy on us.

Incarnate Lord, have mercy on us.

Lover of souls, have mercy on us.

Saviour of sinners, have mercy on us.

Who didst come to seek those that were lost, have mercy on us.

Who didst fast for them forty days and nights, have mercy on us.

By Thy tenderness towards Adam when he fell, have mercy on us.

By Thy faithfulness to Noah in the ark, have mercy on us.

By Thy remembrance of Lot in the midst of sinners, have mercy on us.

By Thy mercy on the Israelites in the desert, have mercy on us.

By Thy forgiveness of David after his confession, have mercy on us.

By Thy patience with wicked Achab on his humiliation, have mercy on us.

By Thy restoration of the penitent Manasses, have mercy on us.

By Thy long suffering towards the Ninevites, when they went in sackcloth and ashes.
Have mercy on us.

By Thy blessing on the Maccabees, who fasted before the battle, have mercy on us.

By Thy choice of John to go before Thee as the preacher of penance, have mercy on us.

By Thy testimony to the Publican, who hung his head and smote his breast, have mercy on us.

By Thy welcome given to the returning Prodigal, have mercy on us.

By Thy gentleness with the woman of Samaria, have mercy on us.

By Thy condescension towards Zacchaeus, persuading him to restitution, have mercy on us.

By Thy pity upon the woman taken in adultery, have mercy on us.

By Thy love of Magdalene, who loved much, have mercy on us.

By Thy converting look, at which Peter wept, have mercy on us.

By Thy gracious words to the thief upon the cross, have mercy on us.

We sinners beseech Thee, hear us.

That we may judge ourselves, and so escape Thy judgment, we beseech Thee, hear us.

That we may bring forth worthy fruits of penance, we beseech Thee, hear us.

That sin may not reign in our mortal bodies, we beseech Thee, hear us.

That we may work out our salvation with fear and trembling, we beseech Thee, hear us.

Son of God, we beseech Thee, hear us.

V. Lamb of God, who takest away
the sins of the world,

R. Spare us, O Lord.

V. Lamb of God, who takest away
the sins of the world,

R. Graciously hear us, O Lord.

V. Lamb of God, who takest away
the sins of the world,

R. Have mercy on us.

V. Christ, hear us.

R. Christ, graciously hear us.

V. O Lord, hear our prayer.

R. And let our cry come unto Thee.

Let us pray:

Grant, we beseech Thee, O Lord, to Thy faithful, pardon and peace, that they may be cleansed from all their offenses, and also serve Thee with a quiet mind, through Christ our Lord.

Amen.

(HERE MAKE YOUR RESOLUTIONS FOR AMENDMENT OF LIFE.)

Prayer for Amendment of Life

ARCHDEACON HENRI-MARIE BOUDON

All this I am resolved upon, in presence of my God, and the whole court of heaven.

Help me, all ye blessed spirits, who are joyful witnesses of these my holy resolutions: assist me now to make a humble offering of them all before the throne of grace, and join your better prayers with mine, to beg a blessing on them; without which, although I daily water them with penitential tears, they never will increase and bring forth fruit.

I have said: now I begin. Have mercy on me, O God, according to thy great mercy, for such a change comes only from the right Hand of the Highest.

Amen.

– The Contrite and Humble Heart, Section II, Resolutions of Amendment

The Lord's Prayer

Our Father, who art in heaven, hallowed be Thy name. Thy kingdom come. Thy will be done on earth as it is in heaven. Give us this day our daily bread and forgive us our trespasses as we forgive those who trespass against us. And lead us not into temptation, but deliver us from evil. Amen.

Pater noster, qui es in cælis, sanctificétur nomen tuum; advéniat regnum tuum; fiat volúntas tua, sicut in cælo et in terra. Panem nostrum quotidiánum da nobis hódie, et dimítte nobis débita nostra, sicut et nos dimíttimus debitóribus nostris; et ne nos indúcas in tentatiónem, sed líbera nos a malo. Amen.

Psalm 129

De profundis
The Sixth Penitential Psalm

Out of the depths I have cried to thee, O Lord.

Lord, hear my voice. Let thy ears be attentive to the voice of my supplication.

If thou, O Lord, wilt mark iniquities: Lord, who shall stand it.

For with thee there is merciful forgiveness: and by reason of thy law, I have waited for thee, O Lord. My soul hath relied on his word.

My soul hath hoped in the Lord.

From the morning watch even until night, let Israel hope in the Lord.

Because with the Lord there is mercy, and with him plentiful redemption.

And he shall redeem Israel from all his iniquities.

Eastern Christian Hymn from the Feast of St. Mary of Egypt

In thee, O Mother, was carefully preserved what is according to the Image. For having taken up the Cross, thou didst follow Christ, and by so doing, didst teach us to disregard the flesh, for it passeth away, but to care for the soul as an immortal thing.

Therefore, Holy Mary, thy spirit rejoiceth with the Angels.

Act of Contrition

O my God, I am heartily sorry for having offended Thee, and I detest all my sins, because I dread the loss of Heaven, and the pains of Hell;

But most of all because they offend Thee, my God, Who art all good and deserving of all my love.

I firmly resolve, with the help of Thy grace,

To confess my sins, to do penance, and to amend my life.

Amen.

v. Confidence in Divine Mercy

"God is so disposed towards us, as willingly to pardon those who are truly penitent."

Roman Catechism

Meditation on God's Mercy

ST. THÉRÈSE OF LISIEUX

It is not because I have been preserved from mortal sin that I lift up my heart to God in trust and love. I feel that even had I on my conscience every crime one could commit, I should lose nothing of my confidence: my heart broken with sorrow, I would throw myself into the Arms of my Savior. I know that He loves the Prodigal Son, I have heard His words to St. Mary Magdalen, to the woman taken in adultery, and to the woman of Samaria. No one could frighten me, for I know what to believe concerning His Mercy and His Love. And I know that all that multitude of sins would disappear in an instant, even as a drop of water cast into a flaming furnace.

– Story of a Soul, XI Canticle of Love

Psalm 142

Domine, exaudi
The Seventh Penitential Psalm

Hear, O Lord, my prayer: give ear to my
supplication in thy truth: hear me in thy justice.

And enter not into judgment with thy servant:
for in thy sight no man living shall be justified.

For the enemy hath persecuted my soul:
he hath brought down my life to the earth.

He hath made me to dwell in darkness as those
that have been dead of old.

And my spirit is in anguish within me:
my heart within me is troubled.

I remembered the days of old, I meditated
on all thy works: I meditated upon the works
of thy hands.

I stretched forth my hands to thee:
my soul is as earth without water unto thee.

Hear me speedily, O Lord:
my spirit hath fainted away.

Turn not away thy face from me,
lest I be like unto them that go down into the pit.

Cause me to hear thy mercy in the morning;
for in thee have I hoped. Make the way known
to me, wherein I should walk: for I have lifted up
my soul to thee.

Deliver me from my enemies, O Lord,
to thee have I fled.

Teach me to do thy will, for thou art my God.
Thy good spirit shall lead me into the right land.

For thy name's sake, O Lord, thou wilt quicken
me in thy justice. Thou wilt bring my soul out of
trouble.

And in thy mercy thou wilt destroy my enemies.
And thou wilt cut off all them that afflict my soul:
for I am thy servant.

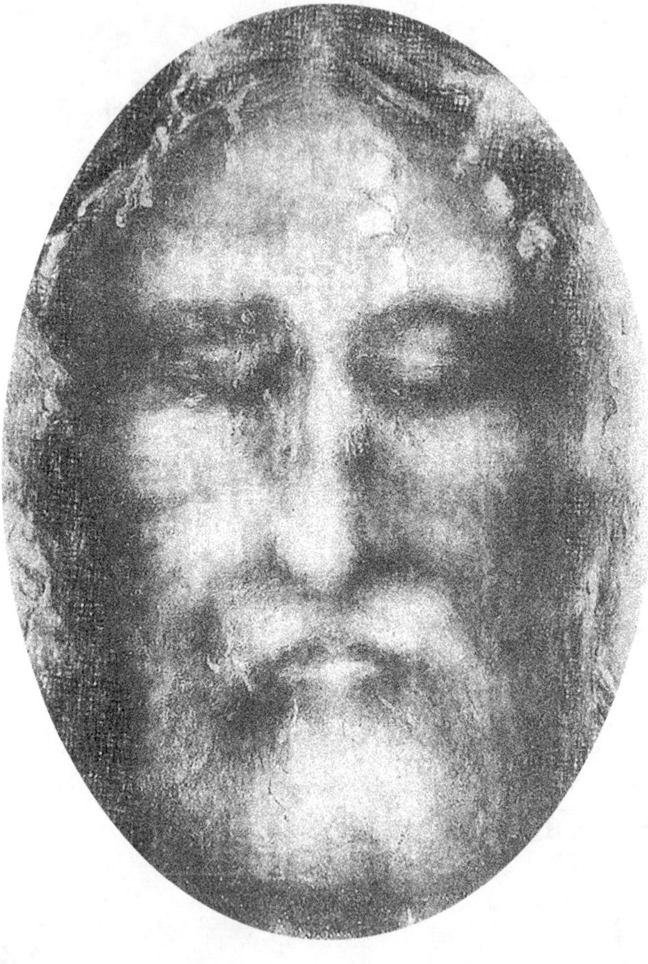

A PRAYER OF CONFIDENCE

VEN. FR. LUIS DE PALMA

Look on one another forever, O Father and Son, look on one another without ceasing, because thus my salvation is secured.

O look of power above nature, O aspect of Divine stars, whence proceed so certainly the rays of Divine grace! When will such a Son disobey? When will such a Father cease to regard His Son? And if the Son obeys, whom will He not love? And if the Father looks on His Son, who shall not be pardoned? Let us then with humble reverence say to Him, whilst presenting to Him His beloved Son, nailed for our sakes upon the Cross, "Look upon us, God our Protector, and regard the face of Thy Christ."

Amen.

– History of the Sacred Passion, pg. 255

IESVS CHRISTVS. SALVATOR MVNDI. REX PACIS

Act of Contrition

O my God, I am heartily sorry for having offended Thee, and I detest all my sins, because I dread the loss of Heaven, and the pains of Hell;

But most of all because they offend Thee, my God, Who art all good and deserving of all my love.

I firmly resolve, with the help of Thy grace,

To confess my sins, to do penance, and to amend my life.

Amen.

VI. Spiritual Communion

"Who will give me wings like a dove and I will fly and be at rest!"

Act of Eucharistic Love

Act of Eucharistic Faith

I firmly believe, O my divine Jesus, that Thou art truly present in the Blessed Sacrament of the Altar. I believe that It really and substantially contains Thy Body and Blood, Thy soul and divinity. I acknowledge these truths; I believe these wonders; I adore the power that has wrought them, the same power that said: "Let there be light," and light was made. Verily, Thou art a hidden God, the God of Israel, the Saviour.

Amen.

Act of Eucharistic Hope

Since Thou vouchsafest to come and dwell within me, O my Redeemer, what may I not expect from Thy bounty! I therefore present myself before Thee with that lively confidence which Thine infinite goodness inspires. Thou not only knowest all my wants, but thou art also willing and able to relieve them. Thou hast not only invited me, but also promised me Thy gracious assistance: "Come to Me all ye that labour and are burdened, and I will refresh you." Behold, then, O Lord, I accept Thy gracious invitation; I lay before Thee all my wants, my misery, and my blindness, and confidently hope, without the fear of being disappointed, that Thou wilt enable me to persevere, unto the end of my life, in Thy service. "In Thee, O Lord, have I hoped: I shall not be confounded forever."

Amen.

Act of Eucharistic Love

As the deer panteth after the fountains of water, so my soul panteth after Thee, O God!

My soul hath thirsted after the strong living God; when shall I come and appear before the face of God?

For what have I in heaven? And besides Thee, what do I desire upon earth?

Let blind and infatuated worldlings intoxicate themselves with the false, transient, and fading happiness of this life; for my part, nothing besides Thyself can content me, either in heaven or on earth.

Come then, O Thou Lamb of God, who takest away the sins of the world!

Come, Thou Beloved of my heart! Adorable Flesh and precious Blood of my Saviour!

Come, to nourish, comfort, and enliven my sickly soul.

O God of my heart! Let me neither love, seek, nor think on any other object but Thyself alone; for Thou alone art my consolation, my treasure, my joy, my life, my all!

My heart and my flesh have rejoiced in the living God.... Thou art, O Lord of hosts, my King and my God! Who will give me wings like a dove and I will fly and be at rest!

Amen.

Spiritual Communion I

ST. ALPHONSUS

My Jesus, I believe that Thou art present in the Blessed Sacrament.

I love Thee above all things and I desire Thee in my soul.

Since I cannot now receive Thee sacramentally, come at least spiritually into my heart.

As though Thou wert already there, I embrace Thee and unite myself wholly to Thee; permit not that I should ever be separated from Thee.

Amen.

Spiritual Communion II

ST. JOSEMARíA ESCRIVÁ

I wish my Lord to receive you, with the purity, humility and devotion with which your Most Holy Mother received you, with the spirit and fervor of the saints.

Amen.

Spiritual Communion III

BYZANTINE CATHOLIC FORM

O Lord, I believe and profess that you are truly Christ, the Son of the living God, who came into the world to save sinners of whom I am the first.

Accept me today as a partaker of your mystical supper, O Son of God, for I will not reveal your mystery to your enemies, nor will I give you a kiss as did Judas, but like the thief I profess you:

Remember me, O Lord,
when you come in your kingdom.

Remember me, O Master,
when you come in your kingdom.

Remember me, O Holy One,
when you come in your kingdom.

May the partaking of your holy mysteries,
O Lord, be not for my judgment or
condemnation but for the healing of soul and body.

O Lord, I also believe and profess that this, which I am about to receive, is truly your most precious body and your life-giving blood, which, I pray, make me worthy to receive for the remission of all my sins and for life everlasting.

Amen.

O God, be merciful to me, a sinner.

O God, cleanse me of my sins
and have mercy on me.

O Lord, forgive me
for I have sinned without number.

Amen.

– Communion Prayer, The Divine Liturgies of Our Holy Fathers John Chrysostom and Basil the Great

Instruction on a Good Thanksgiving

ST. JOSEMARÍA ESCRIVÁ

If we love Christ, who offers himself for us, we will feel compelled to find a few minutes after Mass for an intimate personal thanksgiving, which will prolong in the silence of our hearts that other thanksgiving which is the Eucharist. How are we to approach him, what are we to say, how should we behave? I feel that, on many occasions, the central theme of our conversation with Christ, in our thanksgiving after holy Mass, can be the consideration that our Lord is our king, physician, teacher, and friend.

He is our king. He desires ardently to rule our hearts, because we are children of God. But we should not try to imagine a human sort of rule — Christ does not dominate or seek to impose himself, because he "has not come to be served but to serve."

His kingdom is one of peace, of joy, of justice. Christ our king does not expect us to spend our time in abstract reasoning; he expects deeds, because "not everyone who says to me, Lord, Lord!, shall enter the kingdom of heaven; but he who does the will of my Father in heaven shall enter the kingdom of heaven."

He is our physician, and he heals our selfishness, if we let his grace penetrate to the depths of our soul. Jesus has taught us that the worst sickness is hypocrisy, the pride that leads us to hide our own sins. We have to be totally sincere with him. We have to tell the whole truth, and then we have to say: "Lord, if you will" — and you are always willing — "you can make me clean." You know my weaknesses; I feel these symptoms; I suffer from these failings. We show him the wound, with simplicity, and if the wound is festering, we show the pus, too. Lord, you have cured so many souls; help me to recognize you as the divine physician, when I have you in my heart or when I contemplate your presence in the tabernacle.

He is a teacher, with a knowledge that only he possesses — the knowledge of unlimited love for God, and in God, for all men. In Christ's teaching we learn that our existence does not belong to us. He gave up his life for all men and, if we follow him, we must understand that we cannot take possession of our own lives in a selfish way, without sharing the sorrows of others. Our life belongs to God. We are here to spend it in his service, concerning ourselves generously with souls, showing, through our words and our example, the extent of the Christian dedication that is expected of us.

Jesus expects us to nourish the desire to acquire this knowledge, so that he can repeat to us: "If anyone thirst, let him come to me and drink." And we answer: teach us to forget ourselves, so that we may concern ourselves with you and with all souls. In this way, our Lord will lead us forward with his grace, just as when we were learning to write. Do you remember that childish scrawl, guided by the teacher's hand? And we will begin to taste the joy of showing our faith, which is yet another gift from God, and showing it with clear strokes of Christian conduct, in which all will be able to read the wonders of God.

He is our friend, the Friend: "I have called you friends," he says. He calls us his friends; and he is the one who took the first step, because he loved us first. Still, he does not impose his love — he offers it. He shows it with the clearest possible sign: "Greater love than this no one has, that one lay down his life for his friends." He was Lazarus' friend. He wept for him when he saw him dead, and he raised him from the dead. If he sees us cold, unwilling, rigid perhaps with the stiffness of a dying interior life, his tears will be our life — "I say to you, my friend, arise and walk," leave that narrow life which is no life at all.

– Christ is Passing By, points 92 and 93

Te Deum

We praise thee, O God, we acknowledge thee
to be the Lord.

All the earth doth worship thee
the Father everlasting.

To thee all Angels cry aloud the Heavens,
and all the Powers therein.

To thee Cherubim and Seraphim continually do cry,

Holy, Holy, Holy, Lord God of Hosts; Heaven and earth are full of the Majesty of thy glory.

The glorious company of the Apostles praise thee.

The goodly fellowship of the Prophets praise thee.

The noble army of Martyrs praise thee.

The holy Church throughout all the world doth acknowledge thee;

The Father of an infinite Majesty;

Thine honourable, true and only Son;

Also the Holy Ghost the Comforter.

Thou art the King of Glory O Christ.

Thou art the everlasting Son of the Father.

When thou tookest upon thee to deliver man, thou didst not abhor the Virgin's womb.

When thou hadst overcome the sharpness of death, thou didst open the Kingdom of Heaven to all believers.

Thou sittest at the right hand of God in the glory of the Father.

We believe that thou shalt come to be our Judge.

We therefore pray thee, help thy servants whom thou hast redeemed with thy precious blood.

Make them to be numbered with thy Saints in glory everlasting.

Amen.

In Thanksgiving

O praise the Lord all ye nations. Praise Him, all ye peoples; for His mercy is confirmed upon us, and the truth of the Lord remaineth forever.

V. Let thy people praise Thee, O God.

R. Let all peoples praise Thee.

Let us pray:

O God, our Protector, behold and look upon the face of Thy Christ, Who gave Himself a redemption for all, and grant that from the rising of the sun even to the going down, Thy Name may be great among the Gentiles, and in every place sacrifice and a clean oblation may be offered unto Thy Name. Through the same Christ our Lord.

Amen.

St. Vibiana

“St. Vibiana” by Gwyneth Thompson-Briggs

INNOCENS ATQUE PUDICA
V I B I A N A
ORA + PRO + NOBIS

About St. Vibiana

Saint Vibiana was a virgin martyr who lived and died in third-century Rome. She lived in a time of great persecution, when the strong preyed on the weak, and when many young Christian women were put to death for rejecting the depravity of pagan culture.

We can be certain of little about Saint Vibiana's life, except that it ended with her entrance into Heaven, and this is the most important thing to know about any life. After her martyrdom, early Christians gathered at her tomb to pray and to remember her great purity. Over time, however, she was forgotten. In 1853, her tomb was rediscovered, and her bones were presented to Blessed Pope Pius IX. The Holy Father entrusted these relics to Thaddeus Amat, the soon-to-be Bishop of Los Angeles.

When Bishop Amat arrived in Los Angeles, the city was a violent frontier settlement, only recently conquered by the United States. Amat entrusted the city to Saint Vibiana's patronage, and built a cathedral dedicated to her. Her relics were placed at the main altar. From her position at the heart of the Cathedral, Saint Vibiana watched over generations of Angelenos who came to the Cathedral for baptisms, marriages, funerals, and countless Masses.

Her feast day, September 1st, was observed with great reverence and devotion. Today her bones rest in the crypt of Our Lady of the Angels Cathedral, but her soul stands before God, interceding for Los Angeles, and for all those who call upon her name.

Presented By:

GAUDENT ANGELI

TO GOD THE GREATEST

Gaudent Angeli is committed to revivifying the cult of St. Vibiana, across the land of her patronage, one heart at a time.

To support this apostolate,
visit www.gaudentangeli.com

Bibliography

Holy Bible: Latin Vulgate Translation. Independently Published, 2017.

Boudon, Henri-Marie. *The Contrite and the Humble Heart, with Motives and Considerations for the Preparing of It*. 1801.

Canons and Decrees of the Council of Trent. 1941.

Catholic Church. *The Roman Catholic Daily Missal, 1962*. Baronius Press, 1962.

Catholic Church and Council of Trent. *The Catechism of the Council of Trent*. Tan Books & Pub, 1982.

Escrivá, Josemaría. *Christ Is Passing By*. Scepter Publishers, 2017.

Thérèse of Lisieux. *Story of a Soul*. TAN Books, 2010.

Palma, Luis. *The Sacred Passion*. Scepter Publishers, 2004.

Artwork

GAUDENT ANGELI

TO GOD THE GREATEST

We hereby declare that the devotions and instructions herein contained include such as are sustained by human authority and we submit without reserve to the judgment of the Holy See.

Gaudent Angeli is a 501 (c)(3) nonprofit, and our work is made possible through the generous support of our friends and supporters. We are so grateful for your support in the form of intercessory prayers to our patroness, Saint Vibiana. If you feel called to support our work financially, you may send donations to the address below.

Gaudent Angeli
PO BOX 1015
Claremont, CA 91711

Sophia Institute

Sophia Institute is a nonprofit institution that seeks to nurture the spiritual, moral, and cultural life of souls and to spread the gospel of Christ in conformity with the authentic teachings of the Roman Catholic Church.

Sophia Institute Press fulfills this mission by offering translations, reprints, and new publications that afford readers a rich source of the enduring wisdom of mankind.

Sophia Institute also operates the popular online resource CatholicExchange.com. *Catholic Exchange* provides world news from a Catholic perspective as well as daily devotionals and articles that will help readers to grow in holiness and live a life consistent with the teachings of the Church.

In 2013, Sophia Institute launched Sophia Institute for Teachers to renew and rebuild Catholic culture through service to Catholic education. With the goal of nurturing the spiritual, moral, and cultural life of souls, and an abiding respect for the role and work of teachers, we strive to provide materials and programs that are at once enlightening to the mind and ennobling to the heart; faithful and complete, as well as useful and practical.

Sophia Institute gratefully recognizes the Solidarity Association for preserving and encouraging the growth of our apostolate over the course of many years. Without their generous and timely support, this book would not be in your hands.

www.SophiaInstitute.com
www.CatholicExchange.com
www.SophiaInstituteforTeachers.org